# The
# Essence of Wildness

* * *

# Lessons from Bison

## James A. Bailey

**2016**

**Copies may be ordered from Amazon.com**

**Visit  www.jamesabailey.com**

Printed in the United States

ISBN-10:  0-692-77271-5
ISBN-13:  978-0-692-77271-3

with support from:


**Wildearth Guardians**
**Upper Missouri River Guides**
**Gallatin Wildlife Association**
**William Mealer, MD**
**Yellowstone Buffalo Foundation**

# Table of Contents

# The Essence of Wildness

## Lessons from Bison

**Foreword:** Looking back, I guess I have always been chasing "wildness": as a youngster catching garter snakes and crawdads in Chicago suburbs; and hunting fox squirrels and collecting wild grapes along the back roads of Illinois. Later, I sought wildness canoeing in the Quetico-Superior wilderness; along the still-pristine south shore of Lake Superior; dipping in the Cold River of the Adirondack Preserve; and hiking with students in the Colorado Rockies and the Grand Canyon. These are some of my fondest memories.

Indoors, my reading often led to a wildness that was: The travels of De Vaca, Coronado, and Onate; the journals of Lewis and Clark; diaries of mountain men, Hudson Bay Company brigade leaders, two Jesuit priests, military explorers and other early travelers participating in "manifest destiny".

Wildness was always there to be experienced and savored, yet never captured. But we all have seen wildness diminished, and disappearing essentially forever. Over decades, the process is painfully obvious. In smaller units of time, wildness is lost in almost unnoticeable increments. So I write about how my profession of wildlife management contributes, almost unknowingly, to the loss of wildness.

Many wildlife management practices are applied without thought to effects upon wildness.

My approach is somewhat academic, for I connect wildness of animal populations to population genetics and evolutionary biology. My topics are not new and there is no need to present them in depth with rigorous scientific documentation. For readers needing more detail, the science is available elsewhere in the literature. I believe my contribution lies in connecting these topics within the deductive framework of evolutionary biology to reveal their interacting effects on wildness of wildlife populations.

I focus on large wild mammals, the category I know best and the one most threatened by loss of wildness. Realistically, there remains little room for truly wild populations of many native mammals in temperate North America. Human populations and their alteration of the landscape leave few large, diverse wild habitats necessary to retain truly wild life. Thus, most "wildlife" management must operate with domesticating practices in human-domesticated environments. However, this predominant form of wildlife management fosters neglect of management necessary to retain some wildness. I believe that more and deeper understanding of the meaning and process of wildness can only enhance our perceptions of the values of wildness and of wild country and I propose more recognition of wildness in the practice of wildlife management.

I hope to reach three audiences; practicing wildlife managers, educated laypersons, and students of wildlife management and conservation biology. This goal dictates a simple writing style and format. Some redundancy is necessary to indicate the many interactions among several processes of population genetics. I have found many wildlife managers to react defensively. This is no surprise. Most were trained in wildlife management curricula oriented toward intervention and production, not toward wildness. Moreover, they operate in a legal, political and cultural environment rooted in a time when wildness was more an impediment than a value. I hope to reach wildlife managers; but I place my hopes for the future of wildness with the concerned public and with students.

Thanks to Kathryn QannaYahu for formatting a cover and for much technical assistance. I appreciate the contributions of those whose photographs augment the text. Thanks also to several fellow wildlife biologists who commented and provided suggestions on earlier drafts. Some helped immeasurably by demonstrating how difficult it is to communicate "wildness" to wildlife managers who are caught up in a daily battle to fit wildlife into our increasing and ever-more demanding human environment. This project was supported in part by 42 U. S. Code, Chapter 7.

Jim Bailey, 2016, Belgrade, Montana

x

# THE ESSENCE OF WILDNESS

## LESSONS FROM BISON

Long ago, I wrote a book on wildlife management. That was before I explored the management of bison by state and federal agencies. Soon, I learned that "wildlife management", at least in practice, can be an oxymoron – two incompatible words with conflicting meanings.

I was aware that most plains bison exist today in commercial, privately owned herds, managed much like domestic livestock. In the United States, there are more than 250,000 bison in about 4500 commercial herds. Management practices include annual roundups, handling and culling; vaccinations and antibiotics; rotations through fenced pastures; supplemental feeding; maintaining a stable herd size; keeping a skewed sex ratio with an abundance of females; and maintaining a preponderance of young animals. Predation is nonexistent. These and other practices are used to maximize sustainable production of animals for sale.

In contrast, in the United States we have only about 18,000 plains bison in fewer than 50 "conservation herds". These herds are owned and managed by federal, state or local governments; or by two private conservation organizations: The Nature Conservancy and American Prairie Reserve in Montana.

Traveling about the country, I was surprised to learn that domesticating practices used with commercial bison are also common in our conservation herds. In many cases, bison are sold from conservation herds to pay for "conservation" management, explaining use of numerous practices to increase production (Fig. 1).

Fig. 1. The Custer State Park conservation herd of bison is rounded up and processed for handling and culling annually.

Some, mostly federal, conservation herds of bison are managed with less domesticating intervention. Still, annual handling and other interventions occur – necessitated by small, fenced bison ranges, usually located within landscapes dominated by livestock and agriculture where roaming bison are not tolerated. Many conservation herds are in states where laws do not recognize wild bison. Only commercial, domestic bison are allowed under these state laws.

Plains bison in the United States are becoming a domesticated species. Around the world, we have domesticated several species of large mammals in this way, including Asian elephants, both species of camels, Asian wild horses, Asian water buffalo, and yaks. These and other domesticated large mammals are now rare or absent in the wild.

Pondering the domestic vs. wild issue, I wondered: "Is domestication the only future for plains bison in the United States?" What are the characteristics of wildness, anyway? Will there be wild bison for future generations of us? But it occurred to me – we can't leave bison to the future. Bison die, while their genes are passed along. We can only leave the bison genome, all the many forms of genes (alleles) in all the bison, to future generations of us.

That's when wildness, and its definition, converged with the sciences of population genetics and evolutionary biology. Wildness is much more than a mere romantic notion, and far too complex for a bumper sticker.

## ELEMENTS OF EVOLUTIONARY BIOLOGY

### Evolution

Evolution is a change or redistribution of alleles across generations of organisms. Biologists recognize two extremes: macroevolution and microevolution. Most people understand macroevolution as producing new species, usually over geologic time, with mutations and natural selection. However, microevolution is primary to this discussion.

Microevolution is a change of allele frequencies within a species or population during a few to several generations. At this time scale, gene pools of species or populations may change due to 1) rare non-lethal mutations, 2) natural or artificial selection, 3) gene flow between populations, and 4) a process called "genetic drift" which randomly redistributes alleles among animals and slowly diminishes the gene pool by discarding some alleles. (See Appendix 1). These short-term genetic changes can significantly alter important, valuable population characteristics. Microevolution is little perceived and understood among the public and often ignored in wildlife management. Domestication of wild bison is a process of microevolution. But, I believe populations of other large mammals are likewise losing their gene-based wildness, albeit at a slower pace.

## Wildness Defined

Millennia of macroevolution and natural selection produced wild bison. However, microevolution can alter the bison genome within decades. Therefore, a preponderance of natural selection will be necessary to maintain the wild character of bison.

Wildness is the opposite of domestication. However, wild and domestic are not discrete categories. There is a continuum of conditions between wild and domestic (including "semi-wild" and "semi-domestic" Fig. 2). Wildness is an important but oft-ignored characteristic of wildlife.

As used here, the terms *wild*, *domestic*, *natural*, and *artificial* all relate to the *degree* of human interference and intervention with other evolutionary processes. It has been argued that humans, having influenced species' evolutions for a long time, are "natural". The argument is often used to justify human impacts and to ignore possibilities for limiting these impacts. However the differences between wild and domestic, and between natural and artificial – while not discrete – are real. These differences are not trivial in our world where wildness, with its values, is diminishing and disappearing.

*Natural selection is the criterion of wildness. The degree of wildness depends upon the preponderance of natural selection*, over other genome-altering processes, during recent and current generations. (These genome-altering processes are discussed below.) For large mammals, any weakening or replacement of natural selection alters the genome toward domestication – a condition of dependence upon human altered environments and upon management interventions that compensate for inadequacies in the genome-environment relationship.

Preponderance of Natural Selection:
← Decreasing          Increasing →

| Domestic | ↔ | Semi-Domestic | ↔ | Semi-Wild | ↔ | Wild |

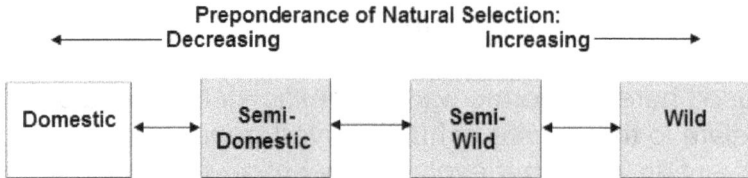

Fig. 2. The domestic-to-wild continuum, here illustrated as four discrete categories. In most wildlife law and in the practice of wildlife management, only two categories are recognized, as all the shaded boxes, shown here, are considered "wild". (In Texas, even the most domesticated animals may be classed as "wildlife".)

For wildlife populations, much of the replacement of, and interference with, natural selection can usually be measured. Consequently, this definition of wildness can be used in the practice of wildlife management.

When Aldo Leopold initiated the profession of wildlife management, wildness was less an issue. The conflict between "wild" and "management" went unnoticed. But as Leopold's ideas matured – even with the limited knowledge of evolutionary biology in his day, he led our profession away from intensive interventions with wildlife and wild places. His guidance becomes increasingly important today as human impacts spread rapidly across the globe. The wildlife profession needs more discussion of wildness. Otherwise, it will participate in diminishing the interesting, awe-inspiring, wondrous and diverse values of wildness, including the ability to adapt to challenges and opportunities of a changing environment.

## The Nature of a Species

Every wildlife species is an adaptive syndrome – a complex set of evolved interacting components that create and define each animal and the species (Fig. 3). These components occur in a hierarchy of 3 layers: characteristics, traits and genes. Here, I use bison to illustrate the complexities within all mammal species.

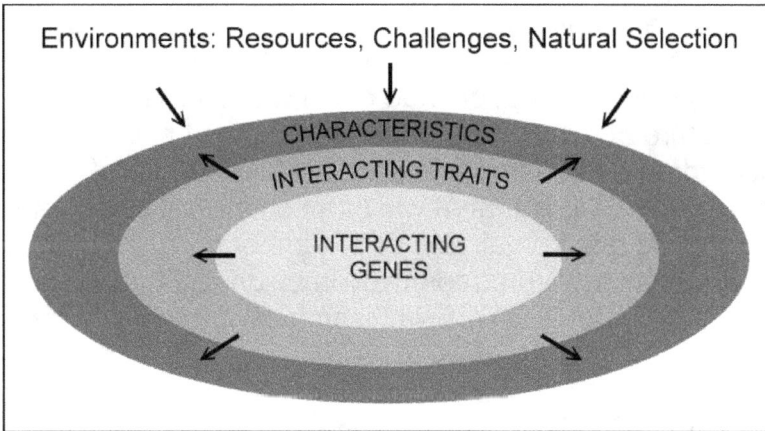

Fig. 3. A Species is far more than what meets the casual eye! Ellipses represent the adaptive syndrome of a species, as described in the text. In turn, the species responds and adapts to the diversity of its environments. Viewed this way, biotic diversity includes taxonomic, genetic and ecotypic variation.

Characteristics are the surface layer of the adaptive syndrome. They are what we see in uncontrolled observations of the animal and its behavior. Important characteristics of wild bison include: mobility, agility, strength, cold-hardiness, energy efficiency, sociality, competitiveness and habitat selection.

Beneath these surface characteristics are anatomical, physiological and behavioral traits of animals. Traits are mostly perceived and understood through controlled studies in a laboratory or pen, or with carefully planned observations of behavior in the field.

Some traits are clearly connected to specific characteristics of animals. Thus, for bison, cold hardiness depends in part upon pelage density for insulation. Bison have about 10 times as many hairs per square inch as do domestic cattle. Cold hardiness also depends upon anatomical and physiological traits that provide bison with a lower critical temperature of minus 40 degrees (Fahrenheit and centigrade are the same at minus 40. A lower critical temperature, LCT, is that at which an animal must increase its metabolic rate to maintain body temperature. An LCT of minus 40 was measured for juvenile bison. LCT is almost certainly lower for a full grown bison having a lower surface area-to-mass ratio.)

The energy efficiency of bison depends, in part, upon its large, complex digestive system, relatively slow rate of food passage, and ability to physiologically recycle nitrogen into the largest stomach where nitrogen limits forage digestion by bacteria. Thus bison digest forage more completely than do domestic cattle.

I have found no comparative anatomy studies, but I predict that bison have especially well-developed cardio-vascular systems ("designed" by natural selection) for rapid, sustained movement. In correlation with this adaptation for mobility, bison calves are precocious, able to move with the herd within hours after birth.

Note that each characteristic of an animal, or species, depends upon several interacting, coordinated traits. In turn, each trait serves several characteristics. Thus a bison's pelage insulates, protects the skin from damage, and visually displays health, fitness and dominance to other bison. Also, the most abundant pelage on the forepart of a bison may have served to deter predator-bites to the most vulnerable parts of the animal – the head, nape and throat.

Beneath animal traits are genetic components: chromosomes, genes in their various forms (alleles), and DNA. This is the least understood layer of the adaptive syndrome of any species (Fig. 4). Much of what we understand of wildlife genetics is inferred from better-studied species and from human genetics.

Science is only beginning to provide a glimmer of the mechanisms and complexity of genetics in relation to animal traits and characteristics. A gene may have more than one effect upon the anatomy, physiology and behavior of its host animal. Some genes must interact with other genes to produce their effects. Thus, the resulting effects upon the host may vary depending upon which combination of alleles is present.

Most importantly, we know that many genes exist throughout a population of animals in slightly different variants (alleles), with slightly different effects. An important population characteristic, allelic diversity, is measured by the variety and frequency of occurrence of different alleles across animals in the population. Allelic diversity determines and limits possibilities for continued evolution. Moreover, allelic diversity contains the results from past evolution. Thus, loss of allelic diversity jeopardizes the benefits from past evolution as well as the evolutionary future.

Fig. 4. Our knowledge of wildlife population genetics is like looking into one window of the Pentagon and trying to deduce what goes on in there (comment from Natalie Halbert, bison geneticist. Photo from wikimedia).

To summarize: In the adaptive syndrome of every species – genes interact to produce traits that interact to produce the many characteristics we observe.

Each species has resulted from evolution and adaptation in, and to, a limited array of habitat conditions that existed during its past. This is the species naturally-associated environment. It is necessary for full expression of a species' adaptive syndrome. For examples, mobility, a core characteristic of the bison adaptive syndrome, cannot occur when bison are confined to limited pastures. Selection for habitats and forages are limited among bison being rotated, like domestic cattle, through a grazing system of often monotonous pastures. The extremes of bison energy efficiency are not used when bison are supplementally fed during severe conditions. Predator escape and defense do not occur without effective predators. Thus, without appropriate environments to elicit evolved responses, some of what a species is, is simply missing. Moreover, there is no continued selection to maintain unused components of the species' adaptive syndrome.

Moreover, the full expression of a species diverse genome may require its existence in a diversity of environments, each with a unique array of environmental resources and challenges that illicit unique responses (ecotypic variation) from the species. Under the Endangered Species Act, we have been largely ineffective in preserving ecotypes of many wild animals.

**Natural Selection: inefficient and conservative**.

While genes carry the message of natural selection across generations, natural selection must operate, not on genes, but at the level of animal characteristics. Characteristics, not genes or even traits, are directly exposed to the selective environment. Characteristics vary among animals according to their innumerably different combinations of alleles. Thus, most natural selection is not efficient in "finding" (favoring or eliminating) the most beneficial or most deleterious alleles. Beneficial alleles may not survive when they occur in an animal with many deleterious alleles (or perhaps in an inbred animal with but a few matched deleterious, recessive alleles). Likewise, deleterious alleles may be retained by occurring with beneficial alleles (or by "hiding" as unmatched, recessive and unexpressed alleles).

Moreover, some forms of natural selection are intermittent, not constant. For example, the values of genes and traits determining extreme energy efficiency would be most favored by natural selection during occasional severe winters. Such selection would be relaxed during mild winters. Alleles determining resistance to specific diseases would be useful only during periodic outbreaks of those diseases.

Further, selection may be periodically reversed. When a population is large in relation to habitat resources, K-selection should favor conservative reproductive strategies (producing a few, highest quality, competitive offspring). When a population declines, or if its habitat is suddenly expanded so that resources are abundant for each animal, r-selection should favor a more risky reproductive strategy (produce as many offspring as possible).

As a consequence of its inefficient and inconstant nature, natural selection is a conservative process that works best with large populations. In large populations, rare alleles are seldom eliminated from all the animals. They are retained in the population's allelic diversity and may again be useful in a changing environment, or as unique sources of future mutations. Conservation biologists have suggested that interbreeding populations of thousands of animals are necessary to maintain their wild genetic integrities. However, the profession of wildlife management has largely ignored this advice.


## Dismantling Wild Genomes

Being inefficient and conservative, natural selection is easily weakened and replaced by seven other evolutionary processes mostly associated with intensive management. These are (1) founder effects: starting new populations with few animals and, consequently, limited allelic diversity; (2) inbreeding; (3) genetic drift due to random events that influence transmission of alleles across generations; (4) outcrossing with other species or varieties of animals; (5) artificial selection: human decisions determining which animals survive and reproduce; (6) failure to maintain gene flow between populations; and (7) management interventions that remove some natural selection from the environment. Five of these processes are discussed in Appendix 1. Two more are described in the next section. These processes are synergistic. Each strengthens and reinforces the others in weakening and replacing natural selection (Fig. 12).

# INTENSIVE WILDLIFE MANAGEMENT: INTERVENING IN NATURAL SELECTION

Many practices, common in intensive wildlife management, create or contribute to some or all the seven processes that weaken or replace natural selection. Effects on wild genomes can only be negative. These practices – most prevalent, almost universal, in management of bison – are becoming more common with other species of large mammals.

**Limited Population Size.** Wildlife populations and their genetic diversities are often limited by the small number of animals available for transplants, by human tolerances for wildlife abundance and distribution, by available forage abundance or responses of vegetation to foraging (sometimes using vegetation standards developed for domestic stock), and for bison, by the sizes of fenced pastures.

For small populations, effectiveness of natural selection is limited by founder effects, inbreeding and genetic drift (Appendix 1); and often by a large proportion of the population being removed or altered with artificial selection and intervention management. These processes, cumulatively, limit both the number and genetic diversity of animals available to natural selection.

As a wild population declines, management interventions such as harvesting, or highway mortality, may not change. Thus, natural selection is replaced for an increasing proportion of the population. Moreover, management may be intensified in response to population decline, further reducing the effectiveness of natural selection.

**Population Stability and Density**. Hunted or culled populations are often managed to maintain stable numbers, often to stabilize production for commercial purposes and/or for recreational harvesting. For controversial large mammals, the concept of a minimally-viable population, MVP, is sometimes invoked, presumably as a compromise with competing interests. Often, the concept of "carrying capacity" is used; but with unclear justification[1]. Moreover, management is often easier to publicly justify when populations and harvestable surpluses fluctuate little among years.

Some bison herds are conservatively maintained at numbers below carrying-capacity – often based on recommendations produced by the federal Natural Resources Conservation Service, an agency focused on the livestock-production concept of carrying capacity. The result is a constant, low ecological density of bison. (Ecological density is the ratio of animal numbers to habitat resources, especially forage, that sustain the animals.)

Stable herds, especially those kept at low ecological density, are less wild because all the natural selection associated with the lowest and especially the highest ecological densities is eliminated. In contrast, wild populations fluctuate in abundance. Natural selection differs between good and bad times and maintains some of the genetic diversity best suited to each. Maintaining a herd at a constant ecological density with its limited, stable assortment of natural

15

selection, fosters what biologists have termed "stabilizing selection". Genetic diversity is diminished by stabilizing selection.

Big game herds are often maintained with stable populations of a moderate size (medium ecological density) that will maximize reproduction and harvestable surpluses. Maintained below the natural limits of their environment, such populations are buffered against episodes of harsh conditions such as food shortages during periods of severe weather or outbreaks of some diseases. Dieoffs of relatively large numbers of animals are rare. However, by eliminating episodes of severe natural selection, the periodic, genetically valuable reduction of deleterious alleles that have accumulated with genetic drift is eliminated. For some big game herds, this effect on the wild genome is exacerbated by supplemental feeding, as noted below.

**Range Size and Diversity**. A diversity of natural selection requires a large and diverse habitat. Monotonous habitats produce limited, monotonous (stabilizing) natural selection.

The great mobility of bison evolved largely (I believe) in response to the advent of human predation in late Ice-age time. Mobility became a core part of the species' evolved strategy for using resources. Most other adaptations of bison must be coordinated with the adaptation of great mobility. On large ranges with vegetative and topographic diversity, bison are adapted for using their mobility to maximize survival and reproduction in response to changing plant phenology and weather conditions. Confining bison to small, monotonous ranges eliminates the evolutionary value of energy-efficient travel and ability to find and use diverse plant and topographic resources. Selection to maintain these important characteristics, and the defining characteristic of mobility, of bison is weakened.

Habitat diversity is diminished for other species of large mammals as well – as human developments consume the landscape. Losses of low-elevation winter ranges, wetlands, and riparian habitats are obvious examples.

**Population Sex-age Structure**. Many conservation herds of bison are managed like most livestock operations, with a skewed sex ratio and a young age structure. Objectives are to maintain a high proportion of growing and producing animals for sale. Whereas wild bison herds normally have near-equal numbers of males and females, some conservation herds have as few as 1 bull per 10 cows. Because a large proportion of the adults are female, many calves are produced annually, and a large proportion of the total herd consists of calves and yearlings. Many yearlings are sold, retaining only a few as replacement breeding animals. Further, breeding-age cows are culled as soon as their prime reproductive years are over. The total result is an abnormally young age structure. With culling of most yearlings and artificial selection of breeding cows and bulls, animals that might have lived the longest, healthiest lives, leaving more calves in the herd, are culled before their genetic contributions are fully realized. Natural selection is thus weakened.

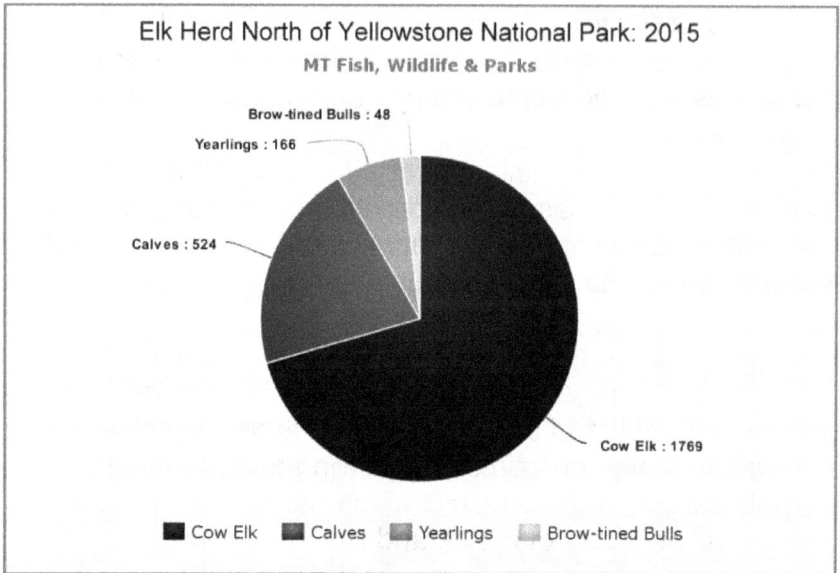

Fig. 5. Many hunted big-game herds are managed with highly skewed sex ratios. In this elk herd, there are only 2.7 mature bulls to breed each 100 cows, producing many half-siblings to interbreed in the next age cohort.

Maintaining a skewed sex-ratio eliminates much of the natural selection associated with bull competition. In the wild, bulls must live and compete well for 6-8 years before becoming dominant breeders. Time and competition, with natural selection, assure that bulls with the best combinations of gene-based characteristics are most represented in subsequent generations. This component of natural selection is weakened in herds with skewed sex ratios.

With other large mammals, intensive hunting that alters

population sex-age structures may weaken natural selection in a like manner. For example, elk herds are often managed with relatively few, mostly young, males. The natural selection of bull aging and competition is lost (Fig. 6) and the limited number of breeding bulls produce many half-siblings, enhancing inbreeding in subsequent generations. This contribution to weakening natural selection is usually discounted by wildlife managers. However, it must be significant in small big-game herds where these effects are combined with inbreeding and genetic drift.

Fig. 6. Competition among male ungulates occurs, not only during the breeding season, but year-round. Such competition, over several years, is a significant arbiter of natural selection determining which males become predominant breeders within their cohort (Jim Coda photograph).

**Disease Management**. Many conservation herds of plains bison are routinely treated with vaccinations, vermicides or antibiotics.

Under wild conditions, host species coevolve with their parasites and diseases. (Some cases involve a 3-way coevolutionary process including an intermediate host species.) Natural selection will favor hosts that avoid infection, minimize infection by physiologically controlling or eliminating disease organisms, or accommodate infection by minimizing its negative effects. These host adaptations can affect relations of the host with more than one species of disease organism simultaneously.

Fig. 7. Wyoming wild elk capture, test and slaughter operation. (Wyoming Game & Fish)

Natural selection will favor disease organisms that are effectively transmitted among hosts, are resistant to physiological control by the host, and are less virulent in that they will not seriously debilitate a host before one or more transmissions to another host can occur.

Clearly, these coevolutionary processes are diverse and complex. They are not well understood. In some cases, coevolution has led to accommodation – that is, from a relationship of parasitism in which the host is harmed toward a relationship of commensalism in which the host is not harmed. Increased disease resistance by the host population and decreased virulence in the disease organisms are to be expected with time.

Interventions with vaccinations, vermicides or antibiotics must interfere with this coevolution. Interventions targeting one disease organism may also weaken coevolution with non-target diseases. Natural selection for host resistance against disease will be weakened or eliminated. Replacing host/disease coevolution with interventions obligates the host population to continuing, often increasing, interventions. Long-term implications of disease intervention management for wildlife have been largely ignored by the wildlife profession. It is time to face and discuss the issue.

**Supplemental Feeding**. About half the conservation herds of bison in the United States are supplementally fed, routinely or during drought or deep-snow conditions.

The practice concentrates animals and facilitates transmission of disease to a degree that would not occur with wild, free-ranging bison. Evolved behaviors for avoiding disease exposure may be impossible. More obviously, supplemental feeding weakens natural selection that would favor competitive animals with the best foraging and energy efficiencies.

Feeding other big-game species in winter is not rare. Deer, especially, are fed by well-meaning individuals who focus on the well-beings of individual animals, not the long-term healths of populations.

Fig. 8. Winter feeding of elk at the National Elk Refuge is a management intervention weakening natural selection that would otherwise favor the most energy- and foraging-efficient animals. (Darius Panahpour Photography)

The largest government sponsored practice of supplementally feeding big game occurs with elk in northwest Wyoming (Fig. 8). However, wintering elk are also fed in Utah, Oregon, Idaho and Washington, and bighorn sheep are fed in Washington. Most or all these programs have strong political backing, based largely in agricultural and other commercial interests. They have been criticized by biologists for many years. A major concern involves enhancement of disease transmission among concentrated animals. Effects, noted here, of dismantling wild genomes have received little attention.

**Routine Handling.** Most conservation herds of bison in the United States are frequently rounded up, penned for days, and processed through handling chutes, much like domestic cattle. Many herds are handled annually. The process facilitates disease management, discussed above, and selective culling, discussed under "Artificial selection" in Appendix 1.

During handling, some animals are injured, even accidentally killed and removed from the gene pool. Less obviously, injured males may acquire reduced abilities to compete for breeding status. At least, these effects contribute to genetic drift. At worst, there may be artificial selection against animals with gene-based behaviors that increase their chances for capture and injury or death during handling.

**Pasture Rotations**. In the United States, about a third of our conservation herds of bison are routinely moved among fenced pastures in rotation systems designed for domestic stock. Human decisions, not gene-based behavior, determine how bison respond to variation in weather and the phenologys of forage plants. Natural selection favoring genes that produce bison making the best decisions is at least weakened.

**Predator Control**. Predation has been a major selective force in evolution of big game species. Many characteristics of big game have been responses, at least in part, to selection by predation. Characteristics such as alertness, agility, mobility and defensive anatomy are obvious results. But other characteristics such as disease resistance, competitiveness, energy efficiency and foraging efficiency have been favored indirectly by predation, as any weakness of any characteristic may increase an animal's risk of predation.

As coursing predators, wolves have been a prominent factor of selection for diverse characteristics of big game fitness. In pursuit, wolves will "test" a group of animals, exposing the weakest individuals (Fig. 9). I suspect wolves are highly sensitive to symptoms of weakness in their prey. Many studies have shown that adult victims of wolf predation tend to be animals debilitated by age, disease or by accidental injuries. These debilitating factors have some genetic bases (as resistance to aging or to disease). Thus, wolves enhance efficiency of natural selection by detecting effects from deleterious alleles, even if these effects are diluted when deleterious alleles occur with beneficial alleles in an animal.

24

Wolves may also participate in coevolution by selectively removing the most virulent strains of pathogens from a prey population.

Fig. 9. A pack of wolves surrounds and outlasts a bison they have chosen as the easiest and safest herd animal to kill.
(Doug Smith, Yellowstone National Park)

Predators often take a heavy toll on newborn and juvenile animals. Compared to killing older animals, such predation may be less selective and more a random contribution to genetic drift. However, even predation on the young may be selective, removing offspring that carry alleles for less precociousness, for mothers that produce weaker young, select vulnerable habitat for birthing, or give birth outside the synchronized birthing period of the herd.

Selective culling by predators has often been described as a "sanitation effect". Emphasis has been upon predator removal of diseased animals. The overall genetic effects of predation are far more complex and have received less attention.

**Highway Mortality.** While not an "intensive management" issue, loss of animals on roads and railroads is a common problem (Fig. 10). These deaths have elements of randomness, contributing to genetic drift, and of artificial selection – in either case replacing natural selection. Impacts of highway mortality upon animal numbers are often recognized. Negative impacts upon evolutionary potentials of populations, especially small populations, are not.

Fig. 10. Roadkills, and hunting, reduce the number of animals available to natural selection, to an important degree for small populations (ucdavis.edu photo).

**Supportive Breeding**. Struggling populations may be demographically supported by removing selected animals, breeding them in captivity, and releasing animals of survivable age back into the population. Careful selection and replacement of breeding animals is necessary to avoid diminishing genetic diversity of the supported population. Even so, natural selection for animals best suited for reproducing in noncaptive conditions is circumvented.

**Loss of gene flow**. Isolated populations, especially small isolated populations, require genetic support from immigrating animals to maintain their genetic diversities, counteracting inbreeding, genetic drift and extinction risk. This tenet of island biogeography, publicized 50 years ago, is often neglected in wildlife management. Some populations

27

are managed to be small. Gene flow between populations is inhibited by loss or degradation of migration corridors, including by highway fences; by any failure to provide highway under- or overpasses for the animals (Fig. 11); or by failure to artificially move animals among populations.

## A Genetically Adequate Wildlife Population

Compared to other North American large mammals, these management practices that interfere with natural selection are by far most pronounced and widely applied with plains bison. However, these practices are not uncommon in today's management of large wild mammals. Many populations are managed with stable, limited population objectives and skewed sex/age structures. Population ranges are diminished in size and diversity as human developments interrupt migration corridors. Predators, including red and Mexican wolves, and regional populations of gray wolves, bears and lions have been reduced or extirpated creating small-population issues for these species. Contributions of their predation to natural selection of their prey are correspondingly reduced or eliminated. Some big-game herds, especially bighorn sheep, are managed with a small-population strategy. A need for constant population interventions signals failure of this strategy. Proposals for managing wildlife diseases with vaccinations, vermicides or antibiotics are becoming common. Emergency or routine feeding of big game occurs, especially for elk. Effects of nearly all these activities on population numbers are recorded and publicized. Effects on population genetic qualities are not.

Fig. 11. Suitable highway overpasses, and underpasses, are increasingly necessary to allow exchange of animals, and facilitate gene flow, among fragmented wildlife populations (WikiPedant/commons.wikimedia).

As a result of the above management practices, or lack of practice, natural selection is often left to operate upon a limited number of animals with a limited genetic diversity *and* natural selection is replaced or weakened with management interventions (Fig. 12). Interventions that reduce exposure of animals to occasional critical conditions weaken selection for alleles that best enable animals to survive and reproduce under such conditions and also weaken the purging of deleterious alleles that accumulate with inbreeding and with genetic drift. The long-term, insidious, synergistic genetic implications of these practices are widely ignored.

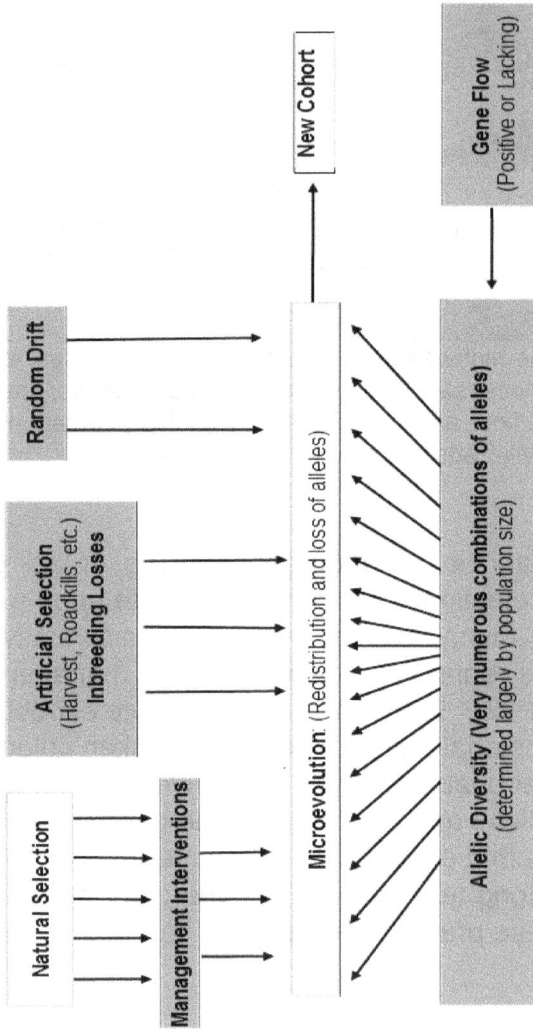

Fig. 12 Simplistic illustration: interaction of allelic diversity with selection processes in one reproductive cycle of a large-mammal population. Shaded areas are much influenced by wildlife management. Allelic diversity is largely a function of population size and number of founders. Gene flow depends upon migration corridors or is artificially managed. Random drift and inbreeding mostly affect small populations. Artificial selection replaces natural selection, whereas management interventions weaken natural selection. In some populations, very few animals are subject to effective natural selection. Across successive reproductive cycles, wildlife management can be the major determinant of genetic quality for a "wild" population.

Lessons From Bison

To encapsulate these ideas: a genetically adequate *wild*life population is large enough to (1) avoid inbreeding and to maintain genetic diversity for (a) retaining wild characteristics bequeathed from past evolution and (b) retaining evolutionary potential for responding to changing environments of the future; and (2) is influenced by a preponderance of natural selection rather than by small population effects and/or by replacement and weakening of natural selection with human interventions and impacts.

A small and declining population of large mammals can be on a spiral of declining genetic adequacy, due to increasing small-population effects and to an increasing proportion of the population being exposed to human interventions that replace natural selection. Unfortunately, the management response is often to intensify intervention management, further diminishing genetic adequacy.

The wildlife management profession should not neglect this issue of wildness. Too many production oriented wildlife managers consider natural selection as a waste, not the source and arbiter of wildness. There is little genetic information to provide a precise evaluation of what values are in jeopardy; but a lack of obvious population symptoms in the short term is no excuse. Allelic diversity is lost and deleterious alleles accumulate rather slowly over generations. At least, caution is justified. Without a preponderance of natural selection, the many admired, valuable wild characteristics of wildlife are at risk.

Paraphrasing Aldo Leopold: The art of population doctoring is being practiced with vigor, but the science of population genetic health is yet rudimentary, and little applied. Perhaps a shift of values can be achieved by reappraising populations that are unnatural, domestic or confined compared to populations that are natural, wild and free.

## WILDNESS IN AMERICA'S FUTURE

### Agency Missions and Wildness
Laws, wildlife agency mission statements and policies ignore or inadequately recognize wildness as a defining or beneficial characteristic of wildlife to be retained for future generations of us.

Most wildlife are managed by the states. Some states recognize both wild and domestic bison with separate sets of laws; but many states do not recognize wild bison at all. Wild animals may be defined in state laws only as those "not reduced to captivity". Most states simply define some species as wild; other species as domestic.

The wildlife management profession, with its outdated legal mandates, largely recognizes wild and domestic only as discrete categories, not as extremes along the wildness continuum (Fig.1). Wild populations are not distinguished according to numbers and intensities of cumulative management interventions that diminish wildness. Generally, any amount and variety of management interventions is acceptable for "wild" populations.

In fisheries management, experience with hatchery-raised fish has forced recognition of the values of wildness. Results from fish hatcheries have been unsatisfactory in developing self-sustaining populations. One state, Montana, decided to emphasize natural reproduction in wild waters for some of its fish species.

Federal laws provide somewhat more recognition of wildness; but often in vague terms. The Wilderness Act refers to wild resources, including wildlife, as "unimpaired in their natural condition" and affected "primarily by the forces of nature". However, habitat impacts from livestock and mining are allowed in wilderness areas. Several interventions of state wildlife management are applied to large-mammal populations that are within, or seasonally within, wilderness areas. Moreover, many wilderness areas are small in relation to the natural movements of large mammals; and some habitat types are poorly represented in the wilderness system.

The Endangered Species Act emphasizes preservation of wildlife numbers, with lesser recognition of population quality, including genetic quality, mostly as recognized in "distinct population segments". Fish and Wildlife Service policy recognizes "elements of natural diversity", avoiding "important losses of genetic diversity" and the "evolutionary legacy" of a species. However, in considering a petition to list wild plains bison as threatened, the Service bypassed the issue of preponderant domesticating activities in bison herds and offered a profound ignorance of the meaning of wildness[2]. In the current political environment, the FWS has difficulty listing species as threatened or endangered based on small and declining population sizes; listing based on the less obvious genetic quality of wildness is unlikely.

FWS has rejected listing considerations for species that have disappeared from major portions, sometimes over 90%, of their historic ranges. The likelihood that unique alleles have disappeared with portions of the range is disregarded and the possibility of losing additional range and genetic diversity is accepted. At the level of genes and alleles, the ESA, at least as currently applied, is woefully inadequate for conserving much little-understood biodiversity.

The National Park Service has the most clear mandate and policies to maintain wildness of resources, including wildlife. NPS' most important statutory directive is to leave natural objects and wildlife unimpaired for future generations. Park policy is to preserve natural resources, processes, systems and values, unimpaired with their inherent integrity perpetuated. Evolution is recognized as a natural process to be minimally influenced by human actions and "natural" is defined as an absence of human dominance. NPS' goal is to maintain the "genetic integrity" of native animal species. However, NPS policy recognizes important limitations. Very many parks are too small to maintain sufficiently large, populations of some mammals and all components of their naturally-associated environments; parks are influenced by activities, including wildlife management, in surrounding landscapes; and Congress may mandate activities that constitute impairment. Furthermore, as our human population grows and parks become increasingly unique on the landscape, there are increasingly effective political pressures to escalate commercial uses that may impair park resources.

## A Future for Wildness?
Most wildlife laws were passed before the complexities of wildness, evolutionary biology and population genetics were revealed by science. As these laws are applied today, they are failing to preserve sufficient examples of wild populations of some large mammals in the contiguous USA. Elsewhere in the world, many other species populations lack genetic adequacy. Results from loss of wildness are accumulating slowly and may not become obvious, or measurable with common techniques, for several generations. But negative results are predictable from modern evolutionary science and have been observed in some populations.

Trends indicate diminishing wildness for more large mammals in the future. To counter these trends, wildlife agencies should reassess their goals and practices to increase accommodations for wildness. Particularly for state wildlife agencies, an infusion of concepts from population genetics and evolutionary biology is needed. Each project of intervention management should be assessed for its necessity and for its probable effects upon the evolved and evolving genetic quality of a wild population. In the USA, small populations of ungulates, bears, wolves, lions, wolverine and fisher are most at risk.

However, much agency intervention will continue to be necessary for wildlife existing within environments that are increasingly modified for human purposes. We have no choice but to foster domestication of wildlife for living in these domesticated environments. Intervention management has its place and it will continue to be common.

Wildness should also have a place. Hopefully, there will be some populations for which the risks of replacing natural selection with commitments to intervention management are recognized and the needs of wildness are accommodated. For this purpose, state wildlife agencies have to expand, their views and practices of wildlife management to embrace a broader range of goals.

Wild populations require large areas of suitable, diverse habitat where there may be a preponderance of natural selection. Wilderness areas and some of our largest national parks were intended to fulfill this need. However, deficiencies of wilderness and parks are cited above. In the contiguous USA, we have large areas of public land where maintenance of wildness could be a primary goal. If such areas were large enough to accommodate the wildness needs of mobile large mammals, the wildness needs of most associated species of plants and animals would also be fulfilled.

Wild animals are fellow travelers on the earth's long road of time. They are part of our inheritance from evolution and from conservationists who have preceded us. They represent a diverse world that is useful, adaptable, interesting and awesome. But wildness is a steadily declining resource in the contiguous USA. We are domesticating and monotonizing our homeland. This trend will not be reversed without a public understanding and appreciation of wildness that generates a will to preserve more and better examples of wildness. In failing to adequately acknowledge and preserve the little-understood but fundamental genetic complexity of wildlife, we are stealing the values of wildness from future generations of us.

# Footnotes

[1] Biological carrying capacity is the number of animals that may be maintained on a sustained basis while achieving specified goals for the population (such as production of young, or of harvestable animals) or for the habitat (such as abundance of certain plant species). Generally, the livestock-management concept of carrying capacity is based on a goal of maximum sustainable and stable production of meat. This narrow concept is often intended but not clearly stated in using the term "carrying capacity" for wildlife populations. Other possible goals for populations or for the vegetation are disregarded.

Social carrying capacity is the number of animals that may be maintained and accepted by one or more social groups, according to their needs and the strengths of their influences upon the wildlife management agency. Often, social carrying capacity is less than biological carrying capacity, though neither is well defined or justified with data when population goals are determined.

[2] In its 2011 decision not to consider listing plains bison under the Endangered Species Act, the Fish & Wildlife

Service stated: "We no longer consider the Yellowstone (Park) herd to have remained in a more wild state than any other conservation herd." This contradicted a 2008 Department of Interior statement, in its Bison Conservation Initiative: "only the Yellowstone herd now meets the criteria for independent long-term genetic conservation (large population size and natural selection)." The absurdity of the 2011 statement lies in equating Yellowstone's large herd, the only conservation herd with a large, diverse range and effective predators, with other conservation herds having numerous practices that weaken or eliminate natural selection. Several of these other herds have fewer than 25 animals in pens smaller than one square mile.

# Appendix

**Founder Effects**. Populations originating from few animals have limited genetic diversity. This limits the ability of natural selection to favor combinations of alleles that would adapt to any environmental change. Like an artist with a limited palette, natural selection has little to work with in small herds.

Around 1890 there may have been fewer than150 plains bison left in North America. They existed in 6 private herds initiated with captured bison from the Great Plains, and perhaps as few as 23 bison left in in the mountains of Yellowstone National Park. Any unique genes from the eastern United States, or from the southern and western Rocky Mountains and westward, were lost. Remarkably, today's bison geneticists have found considerable remaining genetic variation – remaining, but still at risk. Further, we do not know what traits or characteristics have been hampered due to already lost alleles.

Worse, many of the conservation herds of plains bison, relied upon to save the species, have been initiated with very few animals – samples from an already depleted gene pool. We are beginning to recognize this issue of local founder effects as some bison managers exchange animals among herds. But human decisions, not natural selection, choose animals for exchanges.

**Inbreeding**. Breeding between closely related animals enhances the expression of deleterious recessive genes. Inbreeding also increases the probability that beneficial alleles will be "wasted" by being combined with overriding, expressed recessive alleles. This limits the success of beneficial alleles and their chances for survival, under natural selection, across generations.

Simple arithmetic indicates that the frequency of inbreeding will increase as a population becomes smaller. Computer simulations suggest that "significant" levels of inbreeding may occur in populations less than a few hundred mammals.

However, neither the arithmetic nor computer simulations account for outbreeding behavior – avoidance of breeding between closely related animals. We know little about outbreeding behavior in most species and even less about its effectiveness in the smallest populations. Also, the prevalence of deleterious recessive alleles is expected to vary among populations and species according to breeding behavior and population history. Populations once experiencing bottlenecks of abundance have endured levels of inbreeding that exposed some deleterious recessive alleles to elimination by natural selection. If a population recovers, it is more resistant to future bouts of inbreeding.

With this uncertainty, conservative management should maintain herds of at least a few hundred animals to avoid possibly significant levels of inbreeding. However, this mandate becomes largely academic because many more animals are needed to avoid loss of alleles and genetic diversity through genetic drift.

**Genetic Drift**. Aside from natural, or artificial, selection, random events may determine which alleles are transmitted across generations in a process called "genetic drift". Accidents such as being struck by lightning, drowning or being injured in a fall have a random basis, unrelated to at least most characteristics, and genetic constitutions, of animals. More important, during the formation of ova or sperm, only half the alleles of each parent are passed into one offspring – in an essentially random selection process.

In genetic drift, alleles may, by chance alone, gradually increase or decrease in frequency throughout a population. If the population is large, increases tend to balance decreases and there is little change in allele frequencies between generations due to genetic drift. However, randomness becomes a more frequent source of genetic change in smaller populations. (Flipping 30 heads in 40 coin tosses would be unlikely; but 3 heads in 4 coin tosses would not.)

Moreover, in a longer time span with many generations, the probability of an allele declining, by chance, in a set of successive generations becomes larger. Alleles that become rare among animals in the population may decline, by chance, across several generations to zero, reducing genetic diversity and evolutionary potential of small populations.

Thus, for bison, it has been estimated that a population of 2000-3000 animals will lose, due to genetic drift, 5% of its alleles each 100 years. Smaller herds will lose alleles at a faster rate. Rare alleles are most at risk; and we know very little about the functions of these alleles.

In the same manner, genetic drift may weaken natural selection by replacing it with random events. Over generations in small populations, this will enhance an accumulation of some alleles that are most deleterious during severe environmental conditions, weakening a population's ability to withstand episodic severe conditions.

**Outcrossing**. When animals are bred with distantly related individuals, perhaps even different species, genes from recent or ancient evolution are replaced. Plains bison were cross-bred with domestic cattle in perhaps 4 of the 6 herds that escaped elimination of bison before 1900, and there was much more crossbreeding thereafter. Some fertile female cross-bred animals were produced and bred back into the small number of remaining plains bison. Today, over 90% of all plains bison contain some, usually a small amount of, cattle genes.

Bison are not alone with this problem. Outcrossing of wild

forms has occurred with wild turkeys and wild trout and salmon, at least. Deleterious effects upon reproduction or survival of the wild species have been documented. Likely, other negative effects have gone undetected.

**Artificial selection**. Especially in private herds of bison, human decisions determine which animals survive and reproduce, intentionally replacing natural selection and altering the herd genome. Bison are chosen to breed or to be removed based upon their behavior and ease of handling, growth rates, body size and conformation, and success at calving easily.

In recent years, bison have been selected for culling based on their genetic constitutions or their relatedness to other individuals, with an intent to save rare alleles and overall genetic diversity. Selection for rare alleles reduces the population-wide abundance of common alleles, with unknown effects on a herd since we do not know the functions of these alleles. Rare deleterious alleles may be saved at the expense of some common, valuable alleles.

Artificial selection may also be unintended. For example, culling the first animals that come through handling chutes, and retaining the last animals, can unintentionally select animals for behavioral characteristics which are expected to correlate with both anatomical and physiological characteristics. Overall effects on the herd's genome are unknown, but natural selection has been weakened as the arbiter of the herd genome.

In other big-game species, artificial selection occurs with

excessive trophy hunting or other practices that tend to selectively remove animals during their prime-age reproductive years. These animals have demonstrated their abilities to survive and compete. Removing them before the end of their reproductive years weakens or negates effects of natural selection. The problem is greatest in a small population where the fates of a large proportion of animals can be determined by artificial, rather than natural, selection.

Many big game populations have been established by transplanting limited numbers of animals from other, more productive herds. Sometimes, donor herds are selected because they occupy habitats similar to the transplant site. It is presumed that such transplant animals will have accumulated genetic and learned characteristics that will benefit survival and reproduction in the new, but similar habitat. While the presumption has not been well-tested, the conservative approach seems warranted. Unfortunately, such concerns for the genetic characteristics of donor animals are often neglected and the artificial selection of a genome for a new herd has unknown consequences. The issue is magnified when the number of founding animals, the transplanted genetic diversity, is small.

# References

Bailey, J. A. 2013. American Plains Bison: Rewilding an Icon. Sweetgrass Books, Helena, MT.

Hedrick, P. W. 2009. Conservation genetics and North American bison (Bison bison). J. of Heredity.
Leopold, A. 1949. A Sand County Almanac. Oxford University Press, New York.

Lacy, R. C. 2009. Stopping evolution: Genetic management of captive populations. Pp. 58-81 in Amato, R. DeSalle, G., O. A. Ryder and H. C. Rosenbaum. Conservation genetics in the age of genomics. Columbia University Press, NY.

Traill, L. W., B. W. Brook, R. R. Frankham and C. J. A. Bradshaw. 2009. Pragmatic population viability targets in a rapidly changing world. Biological Conservation 143:28-34.

National Park Service laws and policy: Available at: www.nps.gov/aboutus/lawsandpolicies.htm.

Wikipedia Contributors. 2016. [Internet]. Wikipedia, The Free Encyclopedia.
Genetic Drift: http://en.wikipedia.org/wiki/Genetic_drift.
Natural Selection: http://en.wikipedia.org/wiki/Natural_selection.
r/K Selection: http://en.wikipedia.org/wiki/R/K_selection_theory.
Wilderness Act: http://en.wikipedia.org/wiki/Wilderness_Act.
Endangered Species Act:

http:en//wikipedia.org/wiki/Endangered_Species_Act.

**And for those more technically inclined:**

Giglio, R. M., J. A. Ivy, L. C. Jones and E. K. Latch. 2016. Evaluation of alternative management strategies for maintenance of genetic variation in wildlife populations. Animal Conservation, on line prepublication.

Keller, L. F. and D. M. Waller. 2002. Inbreeding effects in wild populations. Trends in Ecology and Evolution. 17:230-241.

MacArthur, R. H. and E. O. Wilson. 1967. The theory of island biogeography. Princeton University Press, NJ.

Perez-Figueroa, A., T Antao, J. A. Coombs and G. Luikart. 2010. Conserving genetic diversity in Yellowstone bison: effects of population fluctuations and variance in male reproductive success in age structured populations. Technical Report, Yellowstone National Park, National Park Service, Wyoming.

# Glossary (focused on large mammals)

**Adaptive syndrome** – The set of evolved, interacting components (genes, traits and characteristics) that create and define each animal and its species.

**Allele** – One of a number of alternative forms of a gene. Within a population, different individuals may have different alleles to represent the same gene (or location on a chromosome). Different alleles are a source of variation of traits among individuals.

> **Deleterious allele** – An allele capable of producing negative effects on the fitness of its organism. To the extent that deleterious alleles are expressed and limit survival and/or reproduction, they tend to be removed from the population genome by natural, or artificial, selection.

> **Recessive allele** – An allele whose expression in its organism is partly or wholly suppressed by the presence of a different allele on the other of a pair of chromosomes (homologous chromosomes). Recessive alleles are fully expressed only when both of the pair of chromosomes contain the same recessive allele.

> **Deleterious recessive allele** – Deleterious alleles may persist in a population genome if they are recessive, as they usually have little or no effect on the organism's characteristics that are exposed to selection.

**Domestic** -- A condition of dependence upon human support or management interventions, or upon human altered environments, altering the genome-environment relationship and reducing the influence of natural selection upon the genome.

**Evolutionary biology** -- Subfield of biology concerned with evolutionary processes that alter genetic compositions of populations over short (microevolution) or long (macroevolution) periods.

**Fitness** – (Darwinian fitness) – The ability to survive and reproduce, thereby leaving a large contribution to the genome of the next generation. In genetic fitness, animals with the "best" combinations of alleles are, through environmental selection, most suited to survive and reproduce with the resources and challenges of an environment. They are the genome most "fitted" to that environment.

**Gene** -- The molecular unit of heredity. The DNA sequence (at one location within a chromosome) that influences development of one or more of an organism's traits.

**Genome** – Total complement of gene-forms (alleles) in an organism, or within all organisms in a population. A population genome is also called a "gene pool".

**Genetic Drift** – Across generations within a population, a change in the frequency of occurrence among individuals, of one or more alleles, that is due to random (non-selective) processes that influence survival and reproduction of animals and the transmission of alleles during meiosis and reproduction.

**K-selection** – A form of natural selection that predominates when a population exists at high abundance relative to the availability of resources to support animals; causing strong competition among individuals. K-selection favors animals that produce fewer, but higher quality, competitive offspring.

**Naturally associated environment** – The kind of environment in which a species has evolved; consequently, the set of environmental opportunities and challenges to which the species is most precisely adapted for survival and reproduction.

**r-selection** – a form of natural selection that predominates when a population exists at low abundance relative to the availability of resources to support animals; so that competition among individuals is relatively insignificant. r-selection favors animals that produce many offspring, frequently, and beginning at a young age.

**Stabilizing selection** – Selection against the most extreme individual genomes, such that genetic diversity of the population decreases or, at least, does not expand. Stabilizing selection is expected when there is strong selection from a narrow and consistent set of environmental conditions.

**Synergistic** – Interacting to produce an effect that is greater than, perhaps different from, the sum of individual effects.

**Wild** -- Influenced by a preponderance of natural selection. The opposite of domestic, although wild and domestic are not discrete categories.

**Wild-domestic continuum** -- A continuous scale of conditions between the most wild and most domestic, including semi-wild and semi-domestic.

# The Essence of Wildness

www.ingramcontent.com/pod-product-compliance
Lightning Source LLC
Chambersburg PA
CBHW060641280326
41933CB00012B/2107